The Cure for
the Common Culture

Telea Johnson Stafford, MBA

Phenixx Marketing and Media,

www.phenixxmarketing.com

telea@phenixx.com

TABLE OF CONTENTS

Medical Disclaimer

Warning:

The side of effects of this book may include gain of vision, color blindness, objects may be more similar than appear, shortening of tolerance, extreme discomfort with the comfortable.

Follow all instructions with care.

CHAPTER 1

It's Time to Talk

The defining point in any relationship starts and sometimes ends with these four words...*"We Need to Talk."* So, I thought we should start there. Yes, *we need to talk.* It's time for us to have a heart-to-heart discussion about culture, race relations, diversity and inclusion. I know, we have avoided "The Talk" for different reasons while walking past each other, hoping no one would bring it up. We held out for as long as we could. Is it ever the right time? Some have held out for dear life avoiding this conversation from sure lack of interest; others for lack of information, and others because no one wants to be the first one to bring it up with the fear of getting the conversation wrong. I get it. It's taboo to talk about race relations; but in the culture in which we live, it's becoming increasingly more dangerous not to address the elephant in the room for much longer. Well, we could avoid it, but it would be similar to overlooking an illness because in doing so, we may continue to live with something that will eventually overtake us when small insensitivities spread to become full-blown epidemics.

The common culture is everywhere, slipping under boardroom doors, into Human Resources departments and into the sacred halls of politics.

We owe it to ourselves to check ourselves, test our assumptions, and create a healthy awareness of the world; the world that exists outside of our gated, shaded, guarded, homogeneous communities. I am nervous that failure to diagnose the root problem or willingness to ignore the symptoms may increase the levels of under-appreciation and may shake the foundation to the point of no repair.

Telea Johnson Stafford, MBA

Some may disagree with having this worldview on the benefits of a cure for the common culture, but I personally don't care to bear the burden of misinforming our next generation or explaining "why" we looked the other way, if staring it down would challenge the status quo. Even small things challenged, move us forward. Not all may agree, but I believe that every generation has the duty to evolve. In this instance, we are evolving our perspective, and that doesn't come with a handbook, but it does come with this common-sense guide to curing the common culture.

In hindsight, I was kindly coerced into moving to the front of this discussion. I consider myself a strong minded individual only occasionally influenced by the opinions of a few people. A group of my colleagues staged a culture intervention on me (they won't admit to that), and I was pulled aside to have 'the talk.' Yes, the conversation started just like the start of this book. They decided on my behalf that I had sat back and observed for long enough.

I unknowingly (blindspot) had come down with a chill, I'd caught something, likely a case of affluenza (when affluence takes over). I now realize that can happen; affluenza floats in rare air; it appeared that I was contagious. It wasn't a 24-hour bug either, over time I'd been lulled into a successful slumber, i.e. "symptoms." Yes, symptoms can occur to all people, not just white people, majority leaders, and decision makers. No one is immune. And that is how I made my way to writing this book.

First, I went through a process of self-diagnosis. Over time, I was able to identify where I'd accepted bias, and where I'd embraced it, even if it meant that I didn't get a fair shot or give one. I am proud, and proof that embracing diversity is an opportunity for all of us. Shift happens.

The shift in my mindset is a work in progress, but now I pay closer attention and consider myself more conscious, and better aware of my own culture, and my role in influencing others and the role of culture today.

Over the years, I've come to realize that in some instances, I am different from a majority of my colleagues, when I sit in the boardrooms or tee off on the golf course. My professional and personal life

Telea Johnson Stafford, MBA

undergirded by strong academic accomplishments, hard work, notoriety and the ability to assimilate was a key driver of my perspective on culture. I've had the privilege of doing some amazing things throughout my career, and I never realized that my presence was also satisfying a shift in other's perceptions. I humbly accept the truth that the opportunities that have been afforded to me are not available for everyone. It's a badge I wear with honor and a position I don't take for granted. I appreciate that I have been the 'first' in many environments to break down the walls of racial and gender stereotypes. But it saddens me that even after becoming the first to fill many senior roles in major marketing firms, I still have to face the reality that everyone is not ready to accept someone that doesn't share the same ethnicities, beliefs or gender preferences.

I can still remember the receptionist saying, "we've never had a black account director." That was years ago when I heard those words. You would think that everyone in 2018, after experiencing a black president for 8 years, and a woman run for presidential office, would be open to the notion of 'no limits' to those of minority status. You would think...

but it's the remarks of one of my current college students that stands out most. "I can't believe that I have a black teacher," he blurted out as I stood in front of the class, teaching English Composition. Those words, meant as a compliment, immediately caused me to reflect on the earlier years of my professional career. I could go on, but I'll spare you the details by simply saying, the symptoms still do exist today. I realize clearly the opportunities that I have claimed were mostly 'firsts,' and while the doors opened for me in some instances, these opportunities are not as common as they could be for others.

Ok, I will go on a bit further… hey, it's my book. As CEO of my own Marketing firm, I have been in boardrooms and heard people comment, "we've never had a woman in this position" as I took a seat at the table. Often times I'm informed by organizations, even for career days at school, that they'd struggled to find female entrepreneurs to speak and represent. I continue to challenge the notion that it is difficult to find diverse talent. My question is, is it really that difficult or is the pipeline limited because decision makers have limited diverse networks? Are diverse candidates still being overlooked for the opportunities? Both sides of the argument would likely have strong opinions to support intention, however, regardless of the intention, the outcome demonstrates a gap that is not closing.

In order to have a respectful conversation, we must see the mutual benefit of both perspectives, which in business, it is widely researched and supported that diverse organizations outperform industry peers with less diverse senior managers (Mckinsey Delivering through Diversity).

This is not a study with research of why you should; instead, this is a simple common-sense guide to seeing and solving our problem. It's simple. So simple that we could pull a thing or two from kindergarten etiquette to start; don't point fingers, use your words and use context clues to sort out what people are trying to say when they have lost their way or lost you in translation. Like all relationships, this one is not so black and white, no pun intended. It's not simple.

I realized that there was a need to write this book to challenge inherent perceptions with using common sense steps. Often, the biggest challenge with making choices that relate to diversity and culture is that we have a perception problem. Realizing your role is also a perception opportunity, while seeing yourself as a person who plays a significant role in creating and shaping culture is critical. Maybe one day, people will learn as I have, that perception and reality cannot coexist for long, because one is always eventually stronger than the other. This book is about tipping the scale; you choose which way. Let's weigh in.

May I suggest it's time for a visit to the Doctor?

Culture can be fluid, friendly and easy-going; it's a topic for an academic fireside chat or a conversation starter at dinner. But there is another side of culture that shows itself when we don't agree or understand each other, the reality check-up is that this clash of culture can hurt people in a number of different ways.

Telea Johnson Stafford, MBA

The Doctor's Visit

Doctor : Tell me why we're here.

Patient : I don't know what's wrong exactly.

Patient : Blank Stare

Doctor : Hmmm.... How long have you been feeling this way?

Patient: I don't know when the pain started exactly, it was minor at first. I am having a hard time making decisions, or when I make decisions, I wonder if they are right. I feel uncomfortable in different situations. I don't like how it feels when I do this or that…. You know?

Doctor   :   We're going to need to run full tests on you.

Patient :   How long is that going to take?

Doctor   :   (Blank stare)

The Evaluation

My heart races when I visit my doctor, the truth is that visiting the doctor is not high on my list of exciting things to do. I visit the doctor because it's a necessity, and I want to live a long and healthy life. For most of us, it's at a minimum the annual check-up that prompts us to make the appointment. For others, there's a pain or discomfort that they've experienced that has sent them there. For some, the visit is to avoid a risk of contagious breakout, while others visit to prevent a problem. The reasons for going to a professional vary, but we'd probably agree that the process itself sucks.

Who would agree to being poked or prodded, evaluated, tested and diagnosed if the outcome didn't depend on it? If we were smart enough to diagnose everything at home, no trip would be necessary. This is also the reason that doctors can't operate on themselves due to conflict of interest. No matter how educated we are, we all need a professional perspective from time to time, typically after home remedies have been exhausted. How much Tylenol can you take? Ultimately, the doctor's perspective is what we are after.

The good and bad news is that there is no 'Doctor for Diversity' but I believe it's safe to say it's probably needed. Until the day comes when someone becomes certified in this field, we will take a common-sense guide to curing the common culture... *Consider this your checkup.*

CHAPTER 3

Symptoms and Diagnosis

H&M Apologizes for 'Monkey' Image featuring Black Child.   New York Times, January 8, 2018

Dove apologizes for ad: We 'missed the mark' representing black women.
CNN Money, October 17, 2017

Telea Johnson Stafford, MBA

As shocking as it may be to read these headlines, these are the symptoms of a growing problem and divide in our culture. They are also examples of how a simple concept like culture becomes complicated when left up to interpretation. These headlines, protest lines and strings of tweets show us that something, if not everything, is wrong. This is today's reality checkup. The headlines highlight the problem but don't dig into the symptoms fully, because people are challenged to identify what they are. Symptoms include, but are not limited to, the lack of culture, lack of appreciation of culture and minimized role that culture plays. Every month, there are side effects from failed attempts that show that the prescription is wrong. We try to self-medicate by including culture without the proper representation in the decision-making phase, or in the due diligence of a cultural initiative message or product. Many are trying to move the needle through a lack of personal understanding of a group and their pain points, customs or sensitivities. Doing this can quickly tip the scale from cultural inclusion to cultural appropriation.

Similar to self-medicating, it is important to understand our own symptoms as well as the symptoms of others. We should consider and evaluate our 'medical' history before making a fatal move. These symptoms, i.e., lack of understanding of culture, shows up in the decision-making process of major brands and corporations as we see the simplicity of knowledge in poorly crafted advertising campaigns. As you can imagine, there were millions of dollars spent to clean up a public perception nightmare. Can we afford these mistakes? Investing in diversity is not only worth it, some would argue you can't afford not to. McKinsey's latest research reinforces the link between diversity and company performance and suggests how organizations can craft better inclusion strategies for a competitive edge.

However, our perception may tell us otherwise, and the numbers support that our perception hasn't changed as much as the demographics. The below statistics shed light on the state of diversity in the US workforce today and suggest the future.

Telea Johnson Stafford, MBA

1. There are fewer Fortune 500 CEOs who are women (4.1%) than who are named David (4.5%) or John (5.3%) – two single male names outnumber an entire gender. (NY Times)

2. Only 5 out of all Fortune 500 companies have African-American CEOs. (CDC, Diversity Inc.)

3. 40% of people think there's a double-standard against hiring women – both men and women are more likely to hire men over women. (Pew)

4. Men are 30% more likely than women to be promoted from entry level to manager. (Women in the Workplace)

5. Resumes submitted by people with African American-sounding names are 14% less likely to get a call back than those with white-sounding names.
   (Research study by University of Wisconsin)

6. 67% of job seekers said a diverse workforce is important when considering job offers. (Glassdoor)

7. 57% of employees think their companies should be more diverse. (Glassdoor)

8. 41% of managers say they are "too busy" to implement diversity initiatives. (SHRM)

9. 83% of millennials are more actively engaged when they believe their company fosters an inclusive culture – and in 10 years, millennials will comprise nearly 75% of the workforce. (Deloitte)

10. The United States will no longer have any single ethnic or racial majorities by the year 2065. (Pew)

11. For every 10% increase in the rate of racial and ethnic diversity on Senior Executive teams, EBIT rises 0.8%. (McKinsey)

12. Ethnically diverse companies are 35% more likely to outperform their respective national industry medians. (McKinsey)

13. Gender diverse companies are 15% more likely to outperform their respective national industry medians. (McKinsey)

14. Companies reporting highest levels of racial diversity in their organizations bring in nearly 15 times more sales revenue than those with lowest levels of racial diversity. (American Sociological Review)

Telea Johnson Stafford, MBA

So, my point is that we see the symptoms, or don't we? And do we see them all? We are great at identifying problems typically. But what is the diagnosis and cure to help us move freely throughout the world, painless and healthy? First, to pinpoint the problem, we have to find out where it hurts, then heal it.

On my last trip to the doctor, I tried to explain what was going on with me. I started by pointing to where it hurt. I kept reaching for the same area as if demonstrating it more than once was increasingly more helpful in pinpointing the problem. Frustrated that I hadn't been clear, I waited for the doctor to respond. The doctor started to push and pull my wrist without speaking. I thought to myself, *well maybe she didn't hear me correctly because I identified that my problem is in an entirely different area*. Then I felt relief, the squeeze in the wrist was somehow connecting to my leg. Life is like that, so many times where the problem starts is not where the problem shows up. The pressure of this conversation sometimes has us medicating the wrong areas and putting a band-aid over our mouths when the pain may be in our wrist, so to speak. A conversation that we rarely have with each other is to ask, where does it hurt?

Where does it hurt?

- It hurts in the boardrooms. Test your relationships with women in leadership outside of work.

- It aches when decisions are being made on who to hire. Try hiring someone who doesn't look like anyone in the room.

- It's painful when the view that we have of others creates a limiting belief that may have a side effect of oppression. Hire someone or recommend people for any and all levels of opportunity in your organization.

- It's uncomfortable when people think less of you. Work on confidence and delivery.

- It hurts most often when it seems to be incurable. Change takes time, so manage expectations and emotional setbacks with the confidence that small steps will eventually cure the problem

Telea Johnson Stafford, MBA

- It hurts everywhere when we can't contain it. Create teachable moments, and stand up for what you believe in.

Let's look for and point out the symptoms when we see them in our own lives or check the people who can't see them without your lens; like my intervention. Some may disagree, but diversity itself is not the problem, diversity does not hurt, but how we treat it can. Of course, we get wounded in the process of change and growth, remember the expression growing pains? It aches when bad treatment is avoidable, and is excruciating when it is intentional. Is it always intentional? No. Is it always avoidable? Of course not.

And common sense isn't always common.

Our Culture is experiencing Growing Pains.

There's no need to re-visit our History books to see that the changes and progress we have made as a society were necessary. Because once, we lived isolated, segregated and separated, and there was no need or personal benefit to understand what hurt others. Honestly, I cannot confirm that being a good person is going to get you a medal of honor, but you should just want to get over yourself and get on with a bigger, more interesting life. Let's be honest, there is no real fact-based reason for jello either, but no one is harassing them about co-existing.

The resistance that we are working against is our history of independence. Until recently, there has been little reason to understand and evaluate how our sensitivities and goals impact each other, because we are more interdependent than we ever have been. Many view that one person's progress comes at the sacrifice of someone else's. We have made some strides, but there is still a long way to go to create an appreciation that progress for one can advance everyone. All ships rise mentality is hard to visualize until you see it work at great organizations like ESPN, a company that has always embraced a diverse culture of inclusion.

ESPN is not only a powerhouse in the sports world but they also have a strong corporate culture of diversity. However, even a best in class culture wasn't enough for a senior leader who challenged senior leadership to make sure that every open

Telea Johnson Stafford, MBA

position had a slate of diverse candidates. And in the story, as it's told, a hiring manager said, "So let me understand this correctly. Should I hire the best candidate or the diverse candidate?" The CEO responded, "yes." The answer was yes to both questions, hire the best candidate who may also be the diverse candidate. It was a teachable moment that demonstrates where some people miss the problem. A diverse candidate or a female candidate isn't always the second-best option. A symptom can infect a person's choice. The prescription is that the diverse candidate and the best candidate could quite possibly be the same, but we will never know if we frame the discussion incorrectly. There are so many times when we hurt the future of another person or the pride or ego simply because we don't know.

The pain point of our common culture continues to create not only the symptoms but a challenge that alludes us in being able to solve it? Well, it hurts all over. That's the easiest answer. It hurts all over.

Old wounds are more memorable than they are noticeable, and just like with our common culture (deeply rooted), we come to the table, the boardrooms, to our jobs, our positions, to our choices and our decisions based on old wounds - how they healed and how we treated it along the way.

Telea Johnson Stafford, MBA

The Prescription

Doctor : The tests are back.

Patient : *(Longest wait ever)* So, what do you see?

Doctor : It's not what you think. It is how you think. But the good news is that your perspective is curable.

Are you starting to feel dizzy, shortness of breath, blurred vision? So what is the prescription for curing perspective? Perspective may be the hardest thing to cure because it has no noticeable symptoms until of course, you notice them.

Snap out of it and come to yourself man... well, there may just be a major sick day coming on. You're not a bad person; we just needed to get that out of the way before we could tackle the solutions. It's so toxic and limiting, wouldn't you agree? We also have eliminated all the reasons that would point to you or I as being racist (go ahead and breathe and give yourself a hug…) So, well, worth the read, right? By now, you are likely still left with two questions. If I am not a racist:

Why am I still reading this book?

Why does my temperature rise whenever the topic of culture, tolerance, and inclusion start to be discussed?

Well, let's see. Have you ever been with a group of friends and a *slightly* racial joke was said and you didn't know whether to laugh or bury your head in shame? Don't be afraid to admit it; we have all been there. If you think about it, you can most likely recall the twinge in your stomach or tightness in the neck you felt because the subject matter wouldn't be as funny if someone representing that culture were sitting with you. Well, that's the rise in temperature I'm alluding to. It feels like a big white elephant (no pun intended) has entered the room.

It's likely that whenever the symptoms of a culture problem are present, we get stuck without a clear prescription of what to do to tolerate it. Not always sure of what the final diagnosis might be, most people brace for the worst and avoid taking any medicine at all. We embrace one extreme over the other without seeing things with a clear level head. Why jump off a bridge when walking across it may be all that is needed?

My grandmother would very rarely take my mother and uncles to a doctor's appointment. She would actually apply lotions for most injuries, and band-aids only in the most extreme circumstances. Do you have a band-aid mindset? Sometimes a little treatment causes more injury. The prescription is to stop patching ourselves up and just rip the band-aid off. This is a guide to having and hosting the conversations that sometimes are necessary with each other. There is also a recommended dosage of truth and transparency for ourselves.

Don't Read the label. Every culture has a stereotype, and every person has a label. Just like the front of a prescription bottle where there is the name, there is another label that includes the ingredients, the terms of use and things to avoid. Each of us has a name and a label that further explains our story and value. Stop to read the label of others. It wouldn't hurt to ask people about their personal values; find out who they are and what shaped them, find unique qualities in the members of your team beyond business contributions. Sometimes it's really about what you're about that counts.

Lifestyle Change. The starting point to increase our inclusion intelligence is to get used to something we are not used to. Make small adjustments in your lifestyle choices each day with a goal of 60 days. This will increase your exposure to new ideas and create an appetite for change. *Change everything or change something.*

Telea Johnson Stafford, MBA

Exercise your Mind. Testing your assumptions about people, places and things broadens our capacity for new ideas. This tests the things we believe to be true. Do you believe that people from one culture are smarter than others? Starting tomorrow, ask someone new about their college experience, degree choice, or dreams for the future. Start by expanding your mindset.

Check your pulse. If you find yourself in mostly comfortable situations (i.e., always eating lunch with people that look like you), it is highly likely that it is time for a change of pace. In the next boardroom meeting or interview, check your pulse to see if you have a steady even measure, the inverse is that someone in the room does not. In rooms where you are most comfortable, reach out to someone who may be discovering something new for the first time and ease their transition. Pay it forward.

Stretch More. Growth is painful and requires nothing of us except patience. Prepare to grow by stretching and sustaining your willingness to grow until it happens. Once a month, set a stretch goal of inclusion; invite someone new to lunch at the office, ask for candidates who are differently abled, foreign, female, etc. The first few times, you may feel stiff but continue to stretch until you're limber, and the reach can get further and further each month.

Take deep Breaths. Keep in mind that at this point you are in rare air. You're probably the 'first.' The first in your family to move outside of the 'family system' or the first in the C-suite to hire a person who doesn't look like the last 5 managers. Breaking the mold takes more than guts, it takes brains and forward thinking. It also takes deep steady breaths, partly because the altitude of rare air can be thin and if taken in too quickly, change can make you light-headed. The other reason to breathe steadily is because you don't want to find yourself holding your breath. First advantage is the way that powerful people became powerful, trust yourself, steady yourself and breathe - it won't be your last.

Whew, that was heavy! But I am confident you can handle, embrace and apply it. Information is only as good as it is respected and implemented. Information is intended to inspire and provoke you, but the reality is that people only respond to things that they respect.

Telea Johnson Stafford, MBA

You must be willing to respect that there is strong reason that making change is a good thing.

If this book has provoked you, great, the next step is to act. Act upon the questions that you may quietly want to know about yourself and others.

Our values are rooted in our assumptions and only by testing and trying new things do we create new values.

CHAPTER 5

Are you Contagious?

A student in one of my classes shared a story of growing up in a home where dating outside of your race was openly discouraged. In this story, the student went on to say that her mom stressed to her children not to bring home anyone who is black. The student wrapped up the story by sharing her shock when her mom introduced the family to her African-American boyfriend of two years. What shocked the family was that this perspective was

Telea Johnson Stafford, MBA

required for so long that now they weren't prepared for how to think differently. The mom in this story had completely cured herself, after shaping the perspective of her immediate and extended family for thirty years or more, she decided just like that, to change.

It is true that culture gets passed down and passed along just like this every day. In fact, culture is hereditary, and parents are carriers. It is also contagious in corporate environments. This story is an example of how personal experiences and lack of them can limit beliefs until something that you value is worth the growth. It took 30 years, but it was in that very moment that the family realized that their mom's perspective was an effort to contain and protect what she knew. But in her efforts, she was also contagious. In any position of influence where your behavior is monitored and even mirrored, you shape culture. Some carriers are unaware of their role. But in all positions of authority, leadership and influence, we are carriers. Also, people who self-identify as an advocate for any position are carriers too. The cure for the common culture is understanding our position and the role that our choices make in containing and creating a common culture. Carriers have the pressure of influence that impacts, inspire or infects families, corporations, and countries. Are there areas of your life where you are containing or contagious?

Some of us may not realize our role in containing and quarantining, but yes, many of us are carriers. Did you know that billions of people worldwide carry the Staphylococcus Bacteria, the one that causes strep throat? And while these carriers have the traces of the infection in them, the bacteria never make them sick. On that same thought, treating them actually prevents others from getting it. Are you getting it?

I don't want to alarm you, but the common culture cannot be contained...there is a new social contract in America driven by a more blended younger and purpose-driven demographic who have always grown up connected. This new social contract is challenging those who are contagious with outdated perspective. For many, it feels like an epidemic...and in some ways; it is possibly an epidemic of progress. The concept of spreading

Telea Johnson Stafford, MBA

self-interest is nothing new, but now every culture has the same purpose, promoting self-interest for all groups, not just the majority can't be prevented or contained at this point. People now desire purpose over participation, and the truth is that this perspective is a shock to the system of many. The common culture is hardest on those who are still coming to terms with a shared human condition and our growing interdependence. Containing people and opportunities are symptoms of trying to save ourselves, but the culture of self-preservation only is out of our hands now, and that may be a good thing. People no longer feel the need to limit who they are in order to get ahead, minimizing differences is considered an outdated prescription for co-existing. And because of this new view, those who carry the banner of the old way of thinking are starting to be identified as contagious. Things are changing. And with that change, we may have to mourn the loss of limited and old identities.

For some, the new view is enough to drive your heart rate up, but following the pulse of America, maybe we should consider the following;

- If we could contain and control the common culture, why would we want to?

- What is the cost of containing our own culture and the price that others have to absorb when their culture is quarantined?

- Is your perspective healthy to you and to others?

Of course, the diagnosis for being contagious is not easy to hear, it's kind of like being put in time-out or a very long snowy day that isn't fun after the first 48 hours. But if you have it bad, it may be worth quarantining for as long as needed. Take a minute or a sick day to get used to the new normal, and then choose how to move forward without pushing old beliefs on new thinking. It is a reality check sometimes to realize that no one is waiting for you if you wait too long. After missing 8 seasons of American Idol, I just realized the other day that the show is still on air. Reality moves on with or without us, and it's funny how that happens. Whether we accept our diagnosis or reject it completely, the culture is changing.

"Culture impacts, affects and infects everyone. It has, for centuries. Without conversations like this, it has affected our generation, and it's time we take our medicine."

CHAPTER 6

Take your Medicine

Open up and take your medicine. Isn't it funny how many parallels there are between going to the doctor to cure anything, and the process for curing ourselves of limited beliefs about each other? Taking your medicine starts with just 'opening up.' Open up to the possibilities. Open up to differences. Open up to different opinions of others and ingest it. Absorbing the environment is the start. After

Telea Johnson Stafford, MBA

absorbing my view, the goal is to expand our capacity for acceptance and competence.

To get the full effect of the medicine, you must swallow your pride and perceptions. To really show commitment to the cure, we must swallow the things that we don't like about ourselves and the things that we don't like about others. For some, this can go down slowly, so it may be necessary to chase it with something familiar because this medicine takes some getting used to.

But the reason to take a shot of cure-all is because hurt people hurt people, we have heard this before, and the saying holds true. Sometimes you don't realize that your own fear and pain show up in odd places and this applies to majority groups and diverse groups. Many will argue that the majority organizations are the ones who are required to medicate themselves. And while I do agree that the majority organizations owe it, not just to the nation but to themselves to take their medicine, there are also clear indicators that everyone can benefit from a few doses of humility and understanding, chased by a generous dose of growth. To be a truly healthy society, the entire community has to build their immune system. Since this is a new prescription, there may be side effects of taking the steps that may include gain of vision, color blindness, objects may be more similar than appear, shortening of tolerance, extreme discomfort with the comfortable.

Telea Johnson Stafford, MBA

CHAPTER 7

The Cure

I am at the point in the book where I ask, why again are we trying so hard to contain our own culture? Let me reiterate, the cure for the common culture is not containment. It is in the ability to heal ourselves, by slowly increasing our resilience for new ideas, new opinions and becoming comfortable with inspiration from new areas and new leadership. One person's progress is another person's prescription. We need to cure ourselves.

The world is changing, and the strands of sensitivities are enormous. The culture types are complex, the prescriptions are rooted in principles, and the depth of understanding is constantly developing. As the world gets larger, the boardrooms get smaller and the echo chambers are being outnumbered by people with the passion for progress and the immune system to co-exist.

You may identify with one of two categories: Areas of your life evolved by necessity and areas where lessons were learned the hard way. For me, there are some areas where change did come more easily as more exposure and opportunities provided the incentive to change. But for those who are in the majority, there is not always a baked in incentive to grow. The mentality is if it's not perceived as broken, there is not really a need to fix it. Not so. The cure is to change the mentality that it has to be broken before we work on it. Relationship experts recommend that couples start their work before it's in disrepair. We are in a state of symptoms right now but moving to solutions will cure us before it gets to the point of no return. As our world continues to evolve, a common culture is a blend of different people and their interests becoming more and more of the norm.

When the majority groups yielded the majority of the power, made most of the decisions and had a head start on other cultures, it was difficult not to assimilate. The consequence of assimilation was that diversity was diluted.

The cure for the common culture is not just about the quantity but also the quality of the culture, meaning that as we go through our prescription and take the medicine that is necessary, we also realize that we want to cure the quality of our culture by pushing for and pulling in new people and new ideas.

In conclusion, the cure for the common culture is about a lifestyle change that may not cure the problem fully until two generations from now, but the treatment starts with today. The cure starts with getting over your symptoms, getting over yourself and getting used to other people. It's that simple, but it also requires that we test our assumptions that we have of people that limits their roles in the workplace, in the home, and in our personal circles. Long gone are the days of living independently, "us" and "them" is on trend to be extinct, and those who fear the new normal will likely be left behind.

The cure for the common culture is similar to major mass spread epidemics that we used to read about in history books. A long time ago people were infected by things that were fatal, until we treated and improved our immune system. I challenge us to cure ourselves and then we will likely eradicate the problem. Imagine looking back in five or ten years from now and wondering why did we make getting along so complicated. Individual identities and unique qualities can co-exist and that's a good thing.

The cure includes a place where more people are asked for an opinion in order to make better and more informed decisions that don't overlook the interests of important groups who haven't always been represented (LGBT, Women, Differently-Abled, African American). We need different sets of eyes

Telea Johnson Stafford, MBA

on laws and legislation to influence and challenge opinions that make us all more comprehensive in our thinking. We need to forgo personal interests formed in certainty because we can certainly be wrong.

So my cure looks like this; I'm going to continue to ask for opportunities that I deserve and others that I don't deserve yet. In instances where I am denied on merit or old behaviors, I will create the opportunity unilaterally. Once created, I will extend opportunities and consideration to others who look like me and to those who do not. I want to thrive in a culture that's open to people learning and growing with me in the room, and be open if they have questions about my story, my culture, my hair or my skin color. I want to keep the conversation open like in a healthy relationship. We have to move from an arranged marriage mentality where you just have to grow to love each other over time. Instead, the cure for the common culture includes a courtship, getting to know each other. Our likes and dislikes, our discords and goals.

Let's get to know each other.

CHAPTER 8

Maintaining your Health

Being inclusive is a habit, and after we've gone through all of the steps in our prescription, the next is sustaining and maintaining it. How do we maintain our cultural health? If you're like me habits are hard to form and very easy to break, but anything that you do overtime with intentional consistency becomes a new habit and eventually part of your core. For me, my core includes coffee and snickers; it just does...don't judge me. But at one point, I had a huge list of bad habits and decided to make a lifestyle change. I remember making the change,

Telea Johnson Stafford, MBA

as painful as it was, I stopped eating French fries and potatoes a few years back. Do you know how hard it is to go through McDonald's drive-through with three kids and not relapse? There are many times that I wanted to dive into the bag of French fries, but over time, it became easier and eventually became my new identity. I started to identify myself as a person with a healthy lifestyle.

It starts with how we identify and how we see ourselves. When we see ourselves as liberal and open-minded or a person who challenges the norm, then that's what we become. The first part of this book showed us who we are, then framed out our options on who we can be, you are what you maintain from here.

Sometimes in maintaining your health, there will be a tendency to go days, weeks, even years without doing anything differently. Put a note on your calendar that once a month, you're going to do something that challenges you to include, reach out, or to learn something new about another group. It's great to set specific, measurable goals, so you can track what you're doing and how far you've come.

As you start, continue or track your journey use the Culture Check Up pages in this book to track your steps. The more you try, track and modify the more you move towards improving the culture around you. And remember those who learn, teach, so share this book with others in your family, company or social groups to start the conversation. Provided for you are Cure for the Common Culture conversation starters. Congratulations on your honorary PHD in Change, I look forward to the work and admire the willingness to do it.

Culture You Can Do.

- Set a goal to attend a meeting that supports an idea that you never thought you would support

- Attend a church of a different religion/ denomination than your own.

- Hire someone that you're on the fence about but can't express why to others.

- Nominate your company for a Diversity award to see how your company would answer the questions and criteria requested in the process.

Telea Johnson Stafford, MBA

- Set up conversation groups with different affinity groups and also 'attend' them.

- Ask for feedback, if you feel that you can't quite put your finger on the change that may need to be made. Get a coach or an accountability partner, someone who will delight in joining you in the journey to be just a little better to walk a little taller.

Culture You Can Track / Conversation Starters

Culture Journal

- How are you doing? Write out how you feel that you are doing in the areas that you read in this book?

- Are there areas that you believe that you have symptoms of culture pains?

- Where did these symptoms come from in your opinion? Family, friends, environment?

- Am I being (more) inclusive?

- What is stopping me from being more inclusive?

- Have I made an attempt (new attempts) to understand or relate to a person of a different race, culture or gender? Why or Why Not?

- Am I comfortable with the progress being made in our culture?

- Is there more I can do? Do I want to? What is blocking my progress?

Warning:

The side of effects of this book may include gain of vision, color blindness, objects may be more similar than appear, shortening of tolerance, extreme discomfort with the comfortable.

Follow all instructions with care.

Telea Johnson Stafford, MBA

CPSIA information can be obtained
at www.ICGtesting.com
Printed in the USA
LVHW102224020922
727390LV00003B/573

9 781983 209512